Patty & J.C.
Love
Frances & Bill
Christmas 1976

A Friendship Gift

A Friendship Gift

as a token of appreciation

By Perry Tanksley

Allgood Books
BOX 1329
JACKSON, MISSISSIPPI 39205

A Friendship Gift

COPYRIGHT © 1970 BY PERRY TANKSLEY

Fifth Printing 1976

SET UP, PRINTED AND BOUND BY THE
PARTHENON PRESS, 201 8TH AVE., SOUTH,
NASHVILLE, TENN., U.S.A.
RETPR395

A Friendship Gift*

"A friend is one who speaks to you after others don't."

"Make other people like themselves a little better, and I promise you they will like you very well."
—*Chesterfield*

*The editor of this volume has collected his favorite poems and quotes from dozens of sources and when possible, acknowledgment of authorship has been given.

ANGER

"Anger is that feeling that makes your mouth work faster than your mind."

"When a man flies into a rage and is beside himself, he is in bad company and always makes a bad landing."

ARGUMENT

"You can't prove anything in an argument except that you're just as bullheaded as the other fellow."

"When all is said and done, the argument is over. Then quit."

AGREEMENT

"My idea of an agreeable person is one who agrees with me."

—*Disraeli*

"The man who always agrees with you will lie to others also."

AMBITION

"There's plenty of room at the top because many of those who got there fell asleep and rolled off."

"To get your head above the crowd, stick your neck out."

ADVICE

"Advice is something the wise don't need and the fools won't accept."

"If you give advice only when asked for it, you'll give very little advice."

AMERICANS

"Americans didn't all come over on the same ship, but we're all in the same boat."

"We'll never get together as long as Americans want to be in the front of the bus, the back of the church, and the middle of the road."

ANCESTORS

"The man who boasts only of his ancestors belongs to a family that is better dead than alive."

"A miser may be difficult to live with but he makes a fine ancestor."

ATHEISM

"The best reply to an atheist is to give him a good dinner and ask him if he believes there is a cook."
—*Louis Nizer*

"Atheists and agnostics pray when they see no other way out of their trouble."

"The worst moment for the atheist is when he is really thankful and has nobody to thank."

AGEING

"The best thing about getting old is that all those things you couldn't have when you were young, you no longer want."
—*L. S. McCanless*

"The worst thing about growing old is having to listen to a lot of advice from one's children."

"It's one of the ironies of life that when one grows tall enough to reach the jam on the pantry shelf, the craving for jam has left."

"The only way to keep from growing old is to die young."

"The longest period in a woman's life is the ten years between the time she 39 and 40."

THE WORLD IS MINE

Today upon a bus I saw
A lovely maid with golden hair;
I envied her, she seemed so gay,
And I wished I were as fair.
When suddenly she rose to leave
I saw her hobble down the aisle;
She had one foot and held a crutch
But as she passed she smiled.
O God, forgive me when I whine,
I have two feet, the world is mine.
And then I stopped to buy some sweets;
The lad who sold them had such charm
I talked with him; he said to me,
"It's nice to talk with folk like you.
You see," he said, "I'm blind."
O God, forgive me when I whine,
I have two eyes, the world is mine!
Then walking down the street I saw
A pretty child with eyes of blue;
He stood and watched the others play;
It seemed he knew not what to do.
I stopped a moment, then I said,
"Why don't you join the others, Dear?"
He looked ahead without a word
And then I knew he couldn't hear.
O God, forgive me when I whine,
I have two ears, the world is mine.
With feet to take me where I'd go,
With eyes to see the sunset's glow,
With ears to hear what I would know,
O God, forgive me when I whine,
I'm blessed indeed, the world is mine.

—Author unknown

OBEDIENCE

I said, "Let me walk in the fields."
He said, "No, walk in the town."
I said, "There are no flowers there."
He said, "No flowers, but a crown."
I said, "But the skies are black—
There is nothing but noise and din."
And he wept as he sent me back;
"There is more," He said, "there is sin."
I said, "But the air is thick
And fogs are veiling the sun."
He answered, "Yet souls are sick,
And souls in the dark undone."
I said, "I shall miss the light
And friends will miss me, they say."
He answered, "Choose tonight
If I am to miss you or they."
I pleaded for time to be given.
He said, "Is it hard to decide?
It will not seem hard in heaven
To have followed the steps of your Guide."
I cast one look at the fields,
Then set my face to the town,
He said, "My child, do you yield?
Will you leave the flowers for the crown?"
Then into his hand went mine,
And into my heart came He;
And I walk in a light divine,
The path I had feared to see.

—*George Macdonald*

ADVERSITY

"When you are kicked from the rear it means you're in front."

—*Fulton Sheen*

"If you must cry over spilled milk, be sure and condense it."

"If we can accept each adversity of life as a kick in the pants instead of in the face, adversity can become a step up the ladder of success."

ABSENT-MINDED

"Some absent-minded men leaving for work slam their wives and kiss the door."

ALERTNESS

"It's better to be a wide-awake ugly than to be a sleeping beauty."

ABSENCE

"Some people fear God so much they haven't been to church for ten years."

ATTENDANCE

"You should go to church because you aren't too good to come and you aren't too bad to come."

BACHELOR

"The only thing worse than being a bachelor is being a bachelor's son."

"Married men have better halves but bachelors usually have better quarters."

"Most bachelors could marry any woman they please but they don't please any."

BOREDOM

"There are those who pray for eternal life who don't know how to use one rainy afternoon."

"Some people can stay longer in an hour than others can in a week."

BOYS

"A boy is a young person who shouldn't do the things his father did at that age."

"Small boys are washable though most of them shrink from it."

BRAINS

"Even the woodpecker knows the only way to get ahead is to use his head."

BOOKS

"Never lend books—no one ever returns them. The only books I have in my library are those people have lent me."
—*Anatole France*

BOASTING

"It's always easy to fill the shoes of big-headed people."

BETRAYER

"Beware of those who give you red-carpet treatment one day and jerk it out from under you the next day."

BARGIN

"A bargin is a transaction in which each party thinks he is cheating the other."

JUST LET ME SEE ANOTHER DAY

I knelt to pray when day was done.
I prayed, "Dear God, bless everyone.
Lift from each troubled heart the pain
And let the sick be well again."
And then I waked another day
And carelessly went on my way.
The whole long day I didn't try
To wipe a tear from any eye.
I didn't try to share the load
Of any neighbor on my road.
I didn't even go to see
The sick one just next door to me.
Yet once again when day was done
I prayed, "Dear God, bless everyone."
But as I prayed, into my ear,
There came a voice that whispered clear,
"Pause, hypocrite, before you pray;
Whom have you tried to bless today?
God's sweetest blessings always go
To those who serve Him here below."
And then I bowed my head and wailed,
"Forgive me, Lord, for I have failed.
Just let me see another day
And I will live the way I pray."

—*Author Unknown*

THE BRIDGE BUILDER

An old man traveling a lone highway,
Came at the evening cold and gray,
To a chasm vast and deep and wide,
Through which was flowing a sullen tide
The old man crossed in the twilight dim,
The sullen stream held no fears for him
But he turned when safe on the other side
And builded a bridge to span the tide.
"Old man," cried a fellow pilgrim near,
"You're wasting your time in building here.
Your journey will end with the closing day;
You never again will pass this way.
You have crossed the chasm deep and wide,
Why build you this bridge at even-tide?"
The builder lifted his old gray head:
"Good friend, in the path I have come," he said,
"There followeth after me today
A youth whose feet must pass this way.
This stream which has been as naught to me,
To that fair-haired youth may pitfall be.
He, too, must cross in the twilight dim—
Good friend, I am building this bridge for him."
—*Will Allen Dromgoole*

BIBLE
"We'll pass through the most gigantic dust storm in history when all churchmembers at the same time dust off their Bibles."

BREAK-OUT
"Give the average prisoner enough rope and he will skip."

BEARING
"The Bible says to bear one another's burdens, not to bear down on them."

BIRTHDAY
"A birthday is the one time that every woman wants her past forgotten and her present remembered."

BROTHERS
"To say that men are brothers may not sound like a promise of peace to some of us who grew up in a family of boys."

BLAME
"Nothing is all wrong. Even a clock that has stopped running is right twice a day."

BACKSLIDING
"If nine-tenths of you were as weak physically as you are spiritually, you couldn't walk."
—*Billy Sunday*

BRAVERY
"There are times when silence is golden, and there are times when silence is yellow. It is high time the church found out which is which."
—*Roy McClain*

BALDNESS
"Let us not forget a live wire usually burns the insulation off."

CONFLICT

"Keep your eye on the ball, your shoulder to the wheel, your ear to the ground, and your nose to the grindstone. Now try to work in that position."

CONFUSION

"If we wish to make a new world we have the materials ready, the first one was made out of chaos."
—*Robert Quillen*

COMPLAINT

"Some nuts enjoy kicking up a dust and then complaining he cannot see."
—*Willard Sperry*

"What if you're next door telling a hard-luck story when opportunity knocks on your door?"

CHILDREN

"Children are a great comfort in your old age—and they help you reach it faster, too."

"A pat on the back will help build character if it is given often enough, hard enough, and low enough."
—*Fulton Sheen*

"Adolescence is the age at which children stop asking questions, because they know all the answers."

"A brat is a child who acts like your own but belongs to your neighbor."

CONCEIT

"Actually I'm not conceited although everyone agrees I have every reason to be."

"Have you read that intelligent book I wrote entitled, *My Great Humility and How I Attained It!*"

"Most self-made men worship their creator."

"Show-offs are usually shown-up in a show-down."

I MET THE MASTER FACE TO FACE

I had walked life's way with an easy tread,
Had followed where comforts and pleasures led,
Until one day in a quiet place
I met the Master face to face.
With station and rank and wealth for my goal,
Much thought for my body but none for my soul,
I had entered to win in Life's mad race,
When I met the Master face to face.
I had built my castles and built them high
And their domes had pierced the blue of the sky.
I'd sworn to rule with an iron mace
When I met the Master face to face.
I met Him and knew Him and blushed to see
That His eyes full of sorrow were fixed on me,
And I faltered and fell at His feet that day
While my castles melted and vanished away.
Melted and vanished, and in their place,
Naught else did I see but the Master's face;
And I cried aloud, "Oh, make me meet
To follow the steps of Thy wounded feet."
My thoughts are now for the souls of men;
I lost my life but I found it again
E'er since one day in a quiet place
I met the Master face to face.

—Author Unknown

STEADFAST HEART

I've dreamed many dreams that never came true.
I've seen them vanish at dawn;
But I've realized enough of my dreams, thank God,
To make me want to dream on.
I've prayed many prayers when no answer came,
Though I waited patient and long,
But answers have come to enough of my prayers
To make me keep praying on.
I've trusted many a friend that failed,
And left me to weep alone,
But I've found enough of my friends true-blue
To make me keep trusting on.
I've sown many seed that fell by the way
For the birds to feed upon,
But I've held enough golden sheaves in my hands
To make me keep sowing on.
I've drained the cup of disappointment and pain
And gone many days without song,
But I've sipped enough nectar from the roses of life
To make me want to live on.
—*Author Unknown*

CONCEIT

"When a person gets too big for his britches his hat doesn't fit either."

"Conceit makes a little squirt think that he is a fountain of knowledge."

"One's head begins to swell when his mind stops growing."

"When a man starts singing his own praises it is pretty sure to be a solo."

CHURCH MEMBERS

"Some church members are like wheelbarrows; they go only when they are pushed."

"If absence makes the heart grow fonder, think how much some people must love the church."

"Christianity helps us to face the music, even when we don't like the tune."

COMMITTEE

"To be effective, a committee should be made up of three persons. But to get anything done, one member should be sick and another absent."

"A committee of five usually consists of the man who does the work, two others to pat him on the back, and two to bring in a minority report."

"A committee is a group of people who individually can do nothing and who collectively decide nothing can be done."

COLLEGE

"A college education never hurt anyone who was willing to learn something afterward."

COMPLIMENT

"Try praising your wife, even if it does frighten her at first."

—*Billy Sunday*

CRITICISM

"Why criticize your wife's judgment. Look who she married."

"Pick your friends but not to pieces."

"Some people delight in taking their exercise by jumping at conclusions."

CANNIBAL

"A cannibal consulted a psychiatrist because he was fed up with people."

CRACKPOT

"A psycho-ceramic is a crackpot."

CYNIC

"A cynic is a man who, when he smells flowers, looks around for a coffin."
—*H. L. Menchen*

CONVERSATION

"Television has improved conversation. There's less of it."

COUNTRY

"What this country needs more than anything else is fewer people telling this country what it needs more than anything else."

CONSCIENCE

"Some suppose they have a clear conscience when actually they have a poor memory."

CREDIT

"Some church members who give the Lord credit for everything ought to switch to cash."

FAITH

I will not doubt, though all my ships at sea
Come drifting home with broken mast and sails;
I shall believe the Hand which never fails,
From seeming evil worketh good for me;
And though I weep because those sails are tattered
Still will I cry, while my best hopes lie shattered,
"I trust in thee."
I will not doubt, though all my prayers return
Unanswered from the still, white realm above;
I shall believe it is an all-wise Love
Which has refused those things for which I yearn;
And though at times I cannot keep from grieving;
Yet the pure ardor of my fixed believing
Undimmed shall burn.
I will not doubt, though sorrows fall like rain,
And troubles swarm like bees about a hive;
I shall believe the heights for which I strive
Are only reached by anguish and by pain;
And though I groan and tremble with my crosses,
I yet shall see, through my severest losses,
The greater gain.
I will not doubt; well-anchored in the faith,
Like some staunch ship, my soul braves every gale,
So strong its courage that it will not fail
To breast the mighty unknown sea of Death.
Oh, may I cry when body parts with spirit,
"I do not doubt," so listening worlds may hear it,
With my last breath.

—*Ella Wheeler Wilcox*

THAT NIGHT

That night when in Judean skies
The mystic star dispensed its light,
A blind man moved in his sleep
And dreamed that he had sight.
That night when shepherds heard the song
Of hosts angelic choiring near,
A deaf man stirred in slumber's spell
And dreamed that he could hear.
That night when in the cattle stall
Slept child and mother, cheek by jowl,
A cripple turned his twisted limbs—
And dreamed that he was whole.
That night when o'er the new born babe
The tender Mary rose to lean,
A loathsome leper smiled in sleep
And dreamed that he was clean.
That night when to the mother's breast
The little King was held secure,
A harlot slept a happy sleep
And dreamed that she was pure.
That night when in the manger lay
That sanctified who came to save,
A man moved in the sleep of death
And dreamed there was no grave.

—*Author Unknown*

DISCIPLINE

"Some cute-acting children deserve to get a big hand in the right place."

"Some families can trace their ancestors back for 300 years but can't tell you where their children were last night."

"A boy is like a canoe—he behaves better if paddled from the rear."

"Child psychology, like paint, should be applied with a brush."

DRESS

"The latest thing in men's clothing today is women."

DAUGHTER

"If the world beats a path to your door, you probably have a beautiful teen-age daughter."

DADS

"A father wants his son to have all the things he never had when he was a boy, including five "A's" on his report card."

DRINKING

"Drinking whiskey doesn't drown sorrows; it irrigates them."

"The tippler who has 'one for the road' may expect a state trooper for a chaser."

"A loose nut at the wheel isn't as dangerous as a tight one."

DIETING

"Seconds count especially when dieting."

"The best reducing exercise is to move the head slowly from side to side when offered a second helping."

"Diets are for people who are thick and tired of it."

DIVORCE

"The high divorce rate indicates that the modern girl hasn't made up her mind whether to have a man for a hobby or a hubby."

"Matrimony and alimony are the chief causes of divorce."

"In seeking the cause of divorce it should be noted that divorce is always preceded by marriage."

"Divorce usually results when a husband decides he's too good to be true."

"I don't have brothers or sisters but I have three Dads by my first Mom and four Moms by my last Dad."
—*Hollywood Youngster*

DOG

"A Dachshund is half a dog high and a dog-and-a-half long."

DOCTORS

"The neurotic builds castles in the sky. The psychotic lives in them. The psychiatrist collects the rent."

DEBT

"Write something that will live forever—sign a house mortgage."

"Car sickness is that feeling you get every month when the payment falls due."

DEDICATION

"He was such a dedicated concrete mixer that he buried himself in his work."

DUTY

"Don't look for four-leaf clovers when there are weeds in your garden."

THE LAND OF BEGINNING AGAIN

I wish that there were some wonderful place
Called the Land of Beginning Again,
Where all our mistakes and all our heartaches
And all of our poor selfish grief
Could be dropped like a shabby old coat at the door,
And never be put on again.
I wish we could come on it all unaware,
Like the hunter who finds a lost trail;
And I wish that the one whom our blindness had done
The greatest injustice of all
Could be at the gates like an old friend that waits
From the comrade he's gladdest to hail.
We would find all the things we intended to do
But forgot, and remembered too late,
Little praises unspoken, little promises broken,
And all of the thousand and one
Little duties neglected that might have perfected
The day for one less fortunate.
It wouldn't be possible not to be kind
In the Land of Beginning Again;
And the ones we misjudged and begrudged
Their moments of victory here
Would find in the grasp of our loving handclasp
More than penitent lips could explain.
For what had been hardest we'd know had been best,
And what had seemed loss would be gain;
For there isn't a sting that will not take wing
When we've faced it and laughed it away;
And I think that the laughter is most what we're after
In the Land of Beginning Again.
So I wish that there were some wonderful place
Called the Land of Beginning Again,
Where all our mistakes and all our heartaches
And all of our poor selfish grief
Could be dropped like a shabby old coat at the door,
And never be put on again.

—*Louisa Fletcher*

I SHALL NOT PASS THIS WAY AGAIN

The bread that bringeth strength I want to give,
The water pure that bids the thirsty live:
I want to help the fainting day by day;
I'm sure I shall not pass again this way.
I want to give the oil of joy for tears,
The faith to conquer crowding doubts and fears.
Beauty for ashes may I give alway:
I'm sure I shall not pass again this way.
I want to give good measure running o'er,
And into angry hearts I want to pour
The answer soft that turneth wrath away;
I'm sure I shall not pass again this way.
I want to give to others hope and faith,
I want to do all that the Master saith;
I want to live aright from day to day;
I'm sure I shall not pass again this way.
—*Ellen H. Underwood*

DISAGREEMENT
"The best way for a husband to win an argument is to take her in his arms."

DUMBNESS
"Many people who remain silent are only speaking their minds."

DIPLOMACY
"Diplomacy is the knack of letting the other fellow have your way."

"Diplomacy is the art of patting a dog and saying 'nice doggie' while looking for a stick to knock his brains out."

DRIVING
"Horsepower was safer when only horses had it."

EMOTIONS
"Mixed emotions is like watching your mother-in-law back off a cliff in your new Cadillac."

EGOTIST
"You can always tell an egotist, but unfortunately you can't tell him much."

ENEMY
"Speak well of your enemies. After all, you made them."

"Love your enemy—it will drive him nuts."

"Don't bore your friends with your troubles. Tell them to your enemies who will be delighted to hear about them."
—*Olin Miller*

EXPERT
"An expert is a little drip under pressure."

"An expert consists of two parts—a spurt is something under pressure. 'X' is the unknown factor."

EVIL

"In the footprints on the sands of time, some people leave only the marks of a heel."

EXPERIENCE

"Experience is what you get while you are looking for something else."

"The class yell of the school of experience is *Ouch*."

"To tell something you don't know is like coming back from somewhere you haven't been."
—*Vance Havner*

EATING

"A bird in the hand is bad table manners."

EXECUTIVES

"Blessed are those who go around in circles for verily they shall be called big wheels."

"Blessed are those who go off with a bang for verily they shall be called big shots."

ENVY

"People green with envy are ripe for trouble."

"Getting married is a good deal like going to a restaurant with your friends. You order what you want and then when you see what the other fellow got, you wish you had taken that."
—*Clarence Darrow*

EXCUSES

"If the Lord lets it rain on the Judgement Day, a lot of church people are going to miss the service."

"Guess I'd rather, when rain is threatening, be on the hay baler thinking about the church worship in progress than to be at worship thinking about wet hay."

I'M GOING TO FOLLOW YOU

Walk a little plainer, Daddy,
Said a little boy so frail,
For I'm following in your footsteps
And I don't want to fail.
Sometimes your steps are very plain
Sometimes they're hard to see
So walk a little plainer, Daddy,
For you are leading me.
I know that you once walked this way
Many many years ago,
And what you did along the way
I'd really like to know.
For sometimes when I'm tempted,
I don't know what to do,
So walk a little plainer, Daddy,
You know I'm following you.
Someday when I'm grown up
You are like I want to be,
Then I will have a little boy
Who'll want to follow me.
And I would want to lead him right
And help him to be true,
So walk a little plainer, Daddy,
I'm going to follow you.

—*Rudell Stribble*

GOSHEN!

"How can you live in Goshen?"
Said a friend from afar,
"This wretched country town
Where folks talk little things all year,
And plant their cabbage by the moon!"
Said I:
"I do not live in Goshen,—
I eat here, sleep here, work here;
I live in Greece,
Where Plato taught,
And Phidian carved,
And Epictetus wrote.
I dwell in Italy,
Where Michael Angelo wrought
In color, form and mass;
Where Cicero penned immortal lines,
And Dante sang undying songs.
Think not my life is small
Because you see a puny place;
I have my books; I have my dreams;
A thousand souls have left for me
Enchantment that transcends
Both time and place.
And so I live in Paradise,
Not here."

—Edgar Frank

ERROR
"To err is human, but if the eraser wears out before the pencil, you're overdoing it a bit."

EDUCATION
"Money saved on education this year will be spent later on jails and reformatories."

ENCOURAGEMENT
"The safest way to knock the chip off a fellow's shoulder is by patting him on the back."
—*F. P. Jones*

FRUSTRATION
"Frustration is buying a new boomerang and finding it impossible to throw the old one away."

"Frustration is when one Siamese twin wants to join the air force and the other volunteers for the submarine service."

FAULT-FINDING
"If fault-finding were electrified, some people would be powerhouses."

"When looking for faults, use a mirror, not a telescope."

"Correcting faults is like tying a necktie; we can do it easier on ourselves than on anybody else."

"When I was young I resolved not to get married until I met the ideal woman. Some years later I found her but she was looking for the ideal man."
—*Michel Simon*

FLATTERY
"It is ten to one when someone slaps you on the back he is trying to make you cough up something."

"Compliments are like perfume, to be inhaled but never swallowed."
—*C. C. Munn*

FREEDOM
"The only place where one can speak and think and act just as one pleases is in the insane asylum."

FUNERAL
"Before I got religion I disliked my great uncle so much I would not have gone to his funeral. Now I'm willing to go to his funeral anytime."

FANATICISM
"Fanaticism is redoubling your effort when you have forgotten your aim."

"In the religious realm it's easier to restrain a fanatic than to resurrect a corpse."

FAILURE
"The only thing in life achieved without effort is failure."

"Failures come in two varieties, those who cannot do what they are told and those who can do nothing else."

"Rip Van Winkle is the only person who ever became famous by sleeping."

FRIENDS
"Be friendly with the people you know. If it were not for them you'd be a total stranger."

"Friends are those who speak to you after others don't."

FOOTBALL
"Football is a game where two halves make a hole and the fullback goes through."

"He spent $10,000 sending his two sons through college but only got a quarterback and a halfback."

THE TOUCH OF THE MASTER'S HAND

It was battered and scarred, and the auctioneer
Thought it scarcely worth the while,
To waste much time on the old violin,
But he held it up with a smile.
"What am I bid for this old violin?
Who will start the bidding for me?
A dollar, a dollar, who'll make it two?
Two dollars, and who'll make it three?
Three dollars once, three dollars twice,
Going for three," but no;
From the back of the room a gray haired man
Came forward and took up the bow,
Then wiping the dust from the old violin,
And tightening up all the strings,
He played a melody pure and sweet,
As sweet as the angels sing.
The music ceased and the auctioneer
With a voice that was quiet and low
Said, "What am I bid for the old violin?"
And he held it up with the bow.
"A thousand dollars, and who'll make it two?
Two thousand, and who'll make it three?
Three thousand once, three thousand twice,
Going and gone," said he.
The people cheered, but some of them said,
"We do not quite understand,
What changed its worth?" Came the reply,
"The touch of the master's hand."
And many a man with his life out of tune,
And battered and scarred with sin
Is auctioned cheap to a thoughtless crowd,
Much like the old violin.
A mess of pottage, a glass of wine,
A game, and he shuffles along;
He's going once, and he's going twice,
He's going and almost gone.

But the Master comes, and the thoughtless crowd
Never can quite understand
The worth of the soul, and the change that is wrought
By the touch of the Master's hand.
—*Myra Brooks Welch*

A SOLDIERS LAST PRAYER*

Look, God, I've never spoken to you
But now I want to say, "How do you do?"
You see, God, they told me you didn't exist
And like a fool I believed all of this.
Last night from a shell hole I saw your sky
And I figured right then they'd told me a lie.
Had I taken time to see the things you made
I'd have known they weren't calling a spade a spade.
I wonder God if you'd shake my hand,
Somehow I feel that you'll understand.
Funny I had to come to this hellish place
Before I had time to see your face.
Well I guess there isn't much more to say
But I'm sure glad, God, I met you today.
I guess the zero hour will soon be here,
But I'm not afraid since I know you're near.
The signal! Well, God, I'll have to go.
I like you lots, this I want you to know.
Look now, this will be a horrible fight;
Who knows? I may come to your house tonight.
Though I wasn't friendly to you before
I wonder if you'd wait at your door.
Look! I'm crying. Me, shedding tears!
I wish I had known you those many years.
Well, I have to go now, God, goodbye!
Strange, since I met you I'm not afraid to die.

*This poem was found in the pocket of a young American soldier who was slain in North Africa, 1943.

FUTURE

"The best thing about the future is that it comes one day at a time."

FEAR

"The wicked flee when no man pursueth, but they make better time when someone is after them."

FLEAS

"Fleas must face the tragic fact that their children usually go to the dogs."

FORGIVENESS

"Always forgive your enemies. Nothing annoys them more."

FRIENDSHIP

"If you want to get rid of somebody, just tell him something for his own good."

GOSSIP

"World history repeats itself. One's personal history is repeated by the neighbors."

"The difference between gossip and news depends upon whether you heard it or told it."

"People will believe anything you tell them if you whisper it."

"A gossip is a person with a keen sense of rumor."

"Gossip is halitosis of the brain."

"Running up hill and running down people are both bad for the heart."

" 'They say' usually means you and another gossiper."

"Hell for a scandal-monger will be to have a surplus of juicy gossip but no ear to deposit it in."

GROUCHINESS
"Some people seem to have been baptized in vinegar."

"A grouch thinks the world is against him—and it is."

GLOOM
"Some church members look sad enough to belong to the embalmers union."

GENTLEMAN
"A gentleman is always as nice as he sometimes is."

GAMBLING
"An enterprising fool drove his $6,000 Cadillac to Las Vegas and rode back in a $100,000 Greyhound."

"Folks used to make their own clothing on spinning wheels. Now they lose their shirts on them."

"Ministers who take a firm stand against games of chance have no business performing marriage ceremonies."

GRUDGE
"The unfailing mark of a blockhead is the chip on his shoulder."

"Most chips on one's shoulder are from the block above."

GARDEN
"To enjoy a beautiful garden, live next door to one and cultivate your neighbor."

GIVING
"When it comes to giving, some people stop at nothing."

GOAL
"Men, like tacks, are useful if they have good heads and are pointed in the right direction."

I WONDER WHY WE REFUSE

Jesus loved the disinherited
And was drawn to the unwanted.
He cared for the lost, the last, and the least
And befriended the unacceptable.
With untouchables He loved to feast.
Wayward prodigals were drawn to Him
As well as penniless peasants.
And down-and-outers gladly listened
And felt at ease in His Presence.
Without criticizing or condemning
He always saw their point of view
And really understood their loneliness
And understood their sinning, too.
In His Presence miracles occurred.
Addicts of lust were suddenly freed.
Thieves left His Presence to make restitutions,
And embezzlers repented of their greed.
Jesus loved the disinherited!
He restored the immoral to chastity
And opened doors of opportunity
To those who felt no one cared
In the home or church or community.
Jesus rejuvenated and changed people.
He made people feel important,
And offering a creative friendship to them
They were able to reorder their lives
Because of their love for Him.
He won them to Himself alone
And eating with the untouchables,
Men rose up sensing their worthwhileness
And went out as stalwart sons of God,
Cleansed from ignorance and vileness,
And all because He loved the disinherited
And was drawn toward the unwanted.
He still feasts with untouchables.
I wonder why we refuse.

—Perry Tanksley

AROUND THE CORNER

Around the corner I have a friend,
In this great city that has no end;
Yet days go by and weeks rush on,
And before I know it a year is gone,
And I never see my old friend's face,
For life is a swift and terrible race.
He knows that I like him just as well
As in the days when I rang his bell
And he rang mine; we were younger then,
And now we are busy, tired men;
Tired with playing a foolish game,
Tired with trying to make a name.
"Tomorrow," I say, "I will call on Jim,
Just to show I am thinking of him."
But tomorrow comes and tomorrow goes,
And the distance between us grows and grows,
Around the corner, yet miles away—
"Here's a telegram. Jim died today."
That's what we get, and deserve in the end—
Around the corner—a vanished friend.

GOD

"My great concern is not whether God is on our side; my great concern is to be on God's side."

—*A. Lincoln*

GOVERNMENT

"A taxpayer is one who has the government on his payroll."

GENERALIZATION

"No generalization is wholly true, including this one."

—*Disraeli*

GIRLS

"Girls don't marry for better or worse. They marry for more or less."

GRANDCHILDREN

"One of the mysteries of life is how the boy who wasn't good enough to marry your daughter can be the father of the smartest grandchild in the world."

GADGETS

"A scientist attempts to prolong life so we will have time to pay for the gadgets he invents."

HAPPINESS

"Some people bring happiness wherever they go; others whenever they go."

"Never miss an opportunity to make others happy, even if you have to let them alone to do it."

"Just think how happy you'd be if you lost everything you have right now—and then got it back again."

"Since there is so little happiness in the world, we might as well be happy without it."

HUMOR

"A good thing to have up your sleeve is a funny bone."

HYPOCRITES

"Why stay away from church because of hypocrites? There's always room for one more."

"Going to church doesn't make you a Christian any more than going to a garage makes you an automobile."

HINDRANCES

"Most of us carry our own stumbling block around with us; we camouflage it with a hat."
—*Mary Alkus*

HUSBAND

"He was so clever he bought his wife such expensive china that she won't trust him to wash the dishes now."

"Getting a husband is like buying an old house. You don't see it the way it is, but the way it's going to be when you get it remodeled."

HATE

"Hating people is like burning down your own house to get rid of a rat."
—*Harry Emerson Fosdick*

HOME

"Home is where a fellow goes when he is tired of being nice to people."

HARDSHIP

"One of the reasons why you need no special education to be a Christian is that Christianity is an education in itself."
—*C. S. Lewis*

"Like the Negro spiritual says, 'Nobody knows the trouble we see,' but we keep trying to tell everybody."

GOD, YOU HAVE BEEN TOO GOOD

God, you have been too good to me,
You don't know what you've done,
A clod's too small to drink in all
The treasure of the sun.
The pitcher fills the lifted cup
And still the blessings pour,
They over brim the shallow rim
With cool refreshing store.
You are too prodigal with joy,
Too careless of its worth,
To let the stream with crystal gleam
Fall wasted on the earth.
Let many thirsty lips draw near
And drink the greater part!
There still will be too much for me
To hold in one glad heart.
—*Charles W. Stork*

ALONG THE ROAD

I walked a mile with Pleasure;
She chattered all the way,
But left me none the wiser
For all she had to say.
I walked a mile with Sorrow
And ne'er a word said she;
But oh, the things I learned from her
When Sorrow walked with me!
—*Robert Browning Hamilton*

CONFESSION

Last night my little boy confessed to me
Some childish wrong,
And kneeling at my knee
He prayed with tears—
Dear God, make me a man
Like Daddy—wise and strong
I know you can.
Then while he slept
I knelt beside his bed,
Confessed my sins
And prayed with low-bowed head,
"Oh God, make me a child
Like my child here—
Pure, guileless,
Trusting Thee with faith sincere."
—*Andrew Gillies*

THE WATCHER

She always leaned to watch for us,
Anxious if we are late,
In winter by the window,
In summer by the gate;
And though we mocked her tenderly
Who had such foolish care,
The long way home would seem more safe
Because she waited there.
Her thoughts were all so full of us,
She never could forget!
And so I think that where she is
She must be watching yet,
Waiting till we come home to her
Anxious if we are late—
Watching from Heaven's window,
Leaning from Heaven's gate.
—*Margaret Widdemer*

HEIRS

"Take care of your pennies—and the dollars will take care of your heirs and their lawyers."

HEALTH

"The nose is that part of the body which shines, snubs, snoops, and sneezes."

HEREDITY

"Heredity is that which makes the father and mother of teenagers wonder a little about each other."

"The funny thing about heredity and environment is that our parents give us both."

HABIT

"If God had meant for people to smoke he would have turned our noses up instead of down."

"A person pays twice for cigarettes—once when he gets them and second when they get him."

HUMAN

"There is a great deal of human nature in people."
—*Mark Twain*

HAIR

"Men wear their hair in three ways—parted, unparted, departed."

HELPFULNESS

"The best helping hand is found at the end of your own arm."

HYPOCHONDRIA

"The hypochondriac was so sensitive that when he received a bad haircut it put him in bed for a day and a half."

IGNORANCE

"A few years ago I thought I knew all the answers. Now I'm not sure I even understand the questions."

INFLATION
"Children have been so expensive that only the poorest people can afford them."

ILLNESS
"A bad cold is both positive and negative. Sometimes the eyes have it, sometimes the nose."

"You give an organ recital each time you review your aches and ills."

IMPORTANCE
"If we could be bought for what we're worth and sold for what we think we're worth we'd be a hot number on the stock market."

INDUSTRY
"I'd like to compliment you on your work—when will you start?"

"God provides food for every bird but he doesn't toss it into the nest."

"Everything good comes to him who hustles while he waits."

"Spade deeper and dig harder if you want your life to be a bed of roses."

IMPROVEMENT
"You can prove the world is getting better. Welfare recipients drive their new cars to receive their dole and most prison inmates are high school graduates."

IDLENESS
"Even if you are on the right track, you will get run over, if you just sit there."

"Doing nothing is very tiring because you can't stop and take a rest."

THE CRUCIFIXION

When Jesus came to Golgotha
They hanged him on a tree,
They drove great nails through hands and feet
And made a Calvary.
They crowned him with a crown of thorns
Red were His wounds and deep
For those were crude and cruel days
And human flesh was cheap.
When Jesus came to Birmingham,
They simply passed Him by,
They never hurt a hair of Him,
They only let Him die;
For man had grown more tender,
And they would not give Him pain,
They only just passed down the street,
And left Him in the rain.
Still Jesus cried, "Forgive them,
For they know not what they do,"
And still it rained the winter rain
That drenched Him through and through;
The crowds went home and left the streets
Without a soul to see,
And Jesus crouched against a wall
And cried for Calvary.

—*G. A. Studdert-Kennedy*

CROWNED, NOT CRUCIFIED

I stood alone at the bar of God
In the hush of the twilight dim
And faced the question that pierced my heart,
"What will you do with Him?
Crowned or crucified? Which shall it be?"
No other way was offered to me.
I looked on His face so marred with tears
That were shed in His agony;
The look in His kind eyes broke my heart,
'Twas so full of love for me.
"The crown or the Cross," it seemed to say.
"For or against me? Choose thou today!"
He held out His loving hands to me
While His pleading voice pled, "Obey!
Make me thy choice for I love thee so,
And you must decide today."
I wept for joy, "I now crown Thee.
No other way seemed right to me.
I knelt in tears at the feet of Christ
In the hush of the twilight dim
And all that I was or hoped or sought
I surrendered unto Him.
Crowned, not crucified! My heart shall know
No king but Christ who loves me so.
—*Author Unknown*

IDEALS
"Girls with a future wisely avoid men with a past."

INHERITANCE
"The wealthy don't live longer—it just seems that way to eager relatives."

"America needs family trees that will produce more lumber and fewer nuts."

IDEA
"Daylight saving time is founded on the old Indian idea of cutting off one end of the blanket and sewing it on the other end to make the blanket longer."

INTEGRITY
"It is better to follow the straight path than to move in the best circles."

"Creditors are more interested in when we'll come across than when our ancestors did."

ILL MANNERS
"Blunt people with dull minds make cutting remarks."

IGNORANCE
"Most church members think an epistle is the wife of an apostle."

INCOME
"More stay-in and less go-out results in more income and less out-go."

INTOXICANTS
"Whiskey builds business—for the hospitals and undertakers."

"An intoxicated man is one who feels sophisticated but can't pronounce it."

—Vic Knight

"He entered the bar fit as a fiddle but left tight as a drum."

IDEOLOGY

"A Communist is one who borrows your pot to cook your goose in."

JOY

"Remember the steam kettle, though up to its neck in hot water, continues to sing."

JOB

"If you paddle your own canoe, you need not worry about any one rocking the boat."

"Don't worry about the job you don't like—someone else will soon have it."

"Well-digging is the only job left where you start at the top."

"One of the hardest jobs is to keep up the easy payment."

JUDGING

"The sin of judging others is usually a worse sin than the sin we condemn in others."

"Maybe we shouldn't judge others but we are all fruit inspectors for Jesus said, 'By their fruits you shall know them'!"

JUVENILES

"Juvenile delinquency is proving that some parents are just not getting at the seat of the problem."
—*Kenneth Shively*

"Knowing that juveniles spring from adults, we think we also know the origin of juvenile delinquency."

ALL OF THEE

O the bitter pain and sorrow
That a time could ever be
When I proudly said to Jesus,
"All of self and none of Thee!"
Yet He found me, I beheld Him
Dying on the accursed tree
And my feeble heart said faintly,
"Some of self and some of Thee!"
Day by day His tender mercies—
Helpful, healing, full and free,
Brought me lower while I whispered,
"Less of self and more of Thee!"
Higher than the highest heaven,
Deeper than the deepest sea,
Lord; Thy love at last has conquered,
"None of self and all of Thee!"

THE WORLD'S BIBLE

Christ has no hands but our hands
To do His work today;
He has no feet but our feet
To lead men in His Way;
He has no tongues but our tongues
To tell men how He died;
He has no help but our help
To bring them to His side.
We are the only Bible
The careless world will read;
We are the sinner's gospel,
We are the scoffers' creed;
We are the Lord's last message,
Given in deed and word;
What if the type is crooked?
What if the print is blurred?
What if our hands are busy
With other work than His?
What if our feet are walking
Where sin's allurement is?
What if our tongues are speaking
Of things His lips would spurn?
How can we hope to help Him
And hasten His return?

—Annie Johnson Flint

JUSTICE

"Justice is what we get when the decision is in our favor."

—*John Raper*

JUMPING

"Digging for facts is much better than getting one's exercise by jumping at conclusions."

KINDNESS

"When tempted to criticize, remember bees don't make honey and sting at the same time."

"Bread cast upon the water after many days returns usually with butter and jam on it."

"If you are not kind, you are the wrong kind."

"Kindness, like a boomerang, always comes back to us."

"After all is said and done, kindness is the only measurement for true greatness."

"One is only remembered for his kindness or the lack of it."

KNOWLEDGE

"It's what you learn after you know it all that counts."

"You don't have to be listed in *Who's Who* to know what's what."

"Knowledge is awareness that fire will burn; wisdom is remembering the blister."

"Some people know a lot more when you try to tell them something than when you ask them something."

"Much worse than a man who knows it all is one who tells it all."

KNOCKING

"Men, like motors, knock only when there is something radically wrong within."

LAZINESS

"If you have nothing to do, don't do it around here."

"Too many people quit looking for work when they find a job."

"Our church is 100% willing—50% are willing workers and the other 50% are willing to let them."

"If some men's ships did come in, they'd be too lazy to unload them."

"A lazy man is good for two things: good for nothing and no good."

"You can't plow a field by turning it over in your mind."

LIFE

"Let us endeavor so to live that when we come to die even the undertaker will be sorry."
—*Mark Twain*

"The difference between life and love is simple. Life is one fool thing after another and love is two fool things after each other."

"Just when you're successful enough to sleep late, you're so old you always wake up early."

"Just when you're finally promoted to the head of the class, you're usually too decrepit to walk up front."

"Life started from a simple cell and for many, ends up with a simple cell—with bars."

"Experience is a school where a man learns what a big fool he has been." *Josh Billings*

CALVARY

Friendless and faint, with martyred steps and slow,
Faint for the flesh, but for the spirit free,
Stung by the mob that came to see the show,
The Master toiled along to Calvary;
We gibed him, as he went, with houndish glee,
Till his dim eyes for us did overflow;
We cursed his vengeless hands thrice wretchedly,
And this was nineteen hundred years ago.
But after nineteen hundred years the shame
Still clings, and we have not made good the loss
That outraged faith has entered in his name.
Ah, when shall come love's courage to be strong!
Tell me, O Lord—tell me, O Lord, how long
Are we to keep Christ writhing on the cross!
—*Edwin Arlington Robinson*

ALTARS

A man I know has made an altar
Of his factory bench.
And one has turned the counter of his store
Into a place of sacrifice and holy ministry.
Another still has changed his office desk
Into a pulpit desk, from which to speak and write,
Transforming commonplace affairs
Into the business of the King.
A Martha in our midst has made
Her kitchen table a communion table,
A postman makes his daily round
A walk in the temple of God.
To all of these each daily happening
Has come to be a whisper from the lips of God,
Each separate task a listening post,
And every common circumstance a wayside shrine.
—*Edgar Frank*

"Life is much easier than you think. All you have to do is accept the impossible, do without the indispensable, and bear the intolerable."

LOVE
"Love at first sight is often cured by a good second look."

LADY
"A lady is a woman who makes it easy for a man to be a gentleman."

LIBERTY
"Liberty is always dangerous but it is by far the safest thing we have."

"Liberty does not mean I'm free to do as I please. It does mean I'm free to do the good, the helpful, and the true."

"A pedestrian has rights and privileges which he dare not assert in the path of an oncoming vehicle."

LISTENING
"Some talkative people never discover why they were given two ears and only one tongue."

"Things shouted or whispered are usually unfit to be listened to."

LUCK
"I'm a great believer in luck. The harder I work the more of it I seem to have."

—*F. L. Emerson*

LABOR
"Small worries are like gnats; movement and activity disperse them."

—*Gustar*

LAUGHTER

"Laughter is the sensation of feeling good all over and showing it principally in one spot."
—*Josh Billings*

MARRIAGE

"A man and his wife were getting along just fine—until the other day when she decided to return home."

"A marriage ring is a sort of a tourniquet worn on one's finger to stop circulation."

"Marriage begins when you sink in his arms and ends with your arms in the sink."

"The husbands lay down the laws but wives usually repeal them."

"Marriage is a fifty-fifty proposition—he tells her what to do and she tells him where to go."

"Girls tend to marry men likes their fathers. That's why some mothers cry at weddings."

"A perfect husband is one who stands by his wife in troubles she wouldn't have, had she not married."

"The ambition of most girls is to make some man a good husband."

"Marriage teaches many virtues which we wouldn't need had we remained single."

"If our marriage does not prove satisfactory, your name will be cheerfully refunded."

"A honeymoon is the brief period between 'I do' and 'you'd better.'"

"Marriage is one game where two can play and both lose."

"Some women work so hard to make good husbands that they never quite manage to make good wives."

"Marriage is a tedious process of finding out what sort of guy your wife would have preferred."
—*Strickland Gillian*

"Marriage is like the army—everybody complains but you'd be surprised how many re-enlist."

"It's a proven fact that it's much easier to live with two hundred pounds of curves than with one hundred pounds of nerves."

"The best time for a man to assert his authority and let his wife know who is boss, is the first time he gets up the courage."

"It has almost reached the point where marriage is sufficient ground for divorce."

"Very few men realize how far short they fall of perfection until they possess a wife."
—*Jean Kennedy*

"I say a fellow ain't very smart if he can't marry a girl smarter than he is."

MANNERS

"Growing up is the period spent in learning that bad manners are tolerated only in grown-ups."

MENTALITY

"Some minds are like concrete—thoroughly mixed up and permanently set."

MONEY

"Money cannot buy you friends but it gets you a better class of enemies."

"Money isn't everything but it's way ahead of whatever is second best."

"Money talks, all right! It says 'goodbye' to me."

"It's wiser to have your bank in heaven than to have your heaven in a bank."

MEMORY

"Pleasant memories must be arranged for in advance."

MEN

"Cute little monkeys grow up to be big monkeys; cute little pigs grow up to be big pigs; some cute little children grow up to be both."

"A million years from now the earth may be filled with creatures who stoutly deny that they ever descended from men."

NATURE

"Nature is wonderful! A million years ago she didn't know we were going to wear glasses, yet look at the way she placed our ears."

"If God had been here last summer and had seen some things I saw, I am sure He would have thought this upper heaven superfluous."
—*Emily Dickens*

NEIGHBOR

"One way to get ahead of your neighbor is by refusing to keep up with him."

"Somehow the better we are, the better the people are that we meet."

NOTHING

"It's dangerous to try to be number one because it's next to nothing."

NEGLECT

"Most of today's troubles on which we stub our toes are the unpleasant unperformed duties which we shoved aside yesterday."

NERVES

"God may forgive your sins, but your nervous system won't."
—*Alfred Korzybski*

"Why is it when children act a certain way and say certain things it's sin but when their parents act that way it's nerves?"

NAME

"Most of us have our names in the paper only three times in life: when we're too young to read, when we're too dazed to read and when we're too dead to read."

OPTIMIST

"An optimist sees in every disaster an opportunity. A pessimist sees in every opportunity a disaster."

"An optimist is wrong as often as the pessimist but he has a lot more fun."

"There's a bright side to everything. For every man who is saddened by the thought that he can't take it with him, at least twenty relatives are made happy."

"An optimist proclaims that we live in the best of all possible worlds. The pessimist fears that is true."
—*James Cabell*

"An optimist is a fellow who takes the cold water thrown on his idea, heats it with enthusiasm, makes steam and pushes ahead."

"An optimist sees the donut; the pessimist sees the hole. An optimist says the glass is half full; the pessimist says the glass is half empty. An optimist rejoices when he finds a stepping stone; the pessimist complains of a stumbling block."

OPPOSITION

"When you're down and out, something always turns up and it's usually the noses of your friends."
—*Orson Wells*

"Loose characters end up in tight places."

"Most of us carry our own stumbling block around with us; we camouflage it with a hat."
—*Mary Alkus*

OPPORTUNIST

"An opportunist is one who when he finds himself in hot water decides he needs a good bath anyway."

"An opportunist is one who enjoys the scenery when he has to take a detour."

"An opportunist is a woman who finds the wolf at the door and later appears in a new fur coat."

OPPORTUNITY

"If opportunity knocked on some people's heads instead of their doors, she'd get better results."

"It is one of the hardships of life that when one has sufficient knowledge to enjoy a particular sort of existence, the opportunity has invariably passed."
—*A. K. Quilter*

"If fate throws a knife at you there are two ways of catching it—by the blade or by the handle."

ORIGINALITY
"When everyone agrees, there is very little thinking."

OLD AGE
"When one gets too old to set a bad example, he starts giving good advice."

OPTIMISM
"Either make light of your woes or keep them in the dark."

PHILOSOPHY
"Philosophy is a study which enables a man to be unhappy more intelligently."

PRAYER
"Lord, make the bad people good and the good people nice."

PROSPERITY
"Few of us can stand prosperity. Another man's, I mean."
—*Mark Twain*

PRAISE
"Wife, when I think of what you mean to me, it's almost more than I can stand not to tell you."
—*Keith Jennison*

PREACHERS
"Jesus did not say, 'club my sheep' or 'shear my sheep.' He said, 'Feed my sheep.'"

PARENTS
"If you must hold yourself up to your children as an object lesson, hold yourself up as a warning and not as an example."

"It's funny how parents obey their children these days."

PUNCTUALITY

"The trouble with being punctual is that there is nobody there to appreciate it."

POVERTY

"Poverty may be no disgrace but that is the only nice thing you can say about it."

POLITICS

"A political speech-writer has a promising career."

"A politician can't fool all the people all the time; besides, once every four years is enough."

PETS

"It's nice for the children to have pets until the pets start having children."

PRIDE

"Some people are so sensitive that when you pat them on the back their head swells."

"Blessed is he who tooteth his own horn; otherwise it shall not be tooted."

PEOPLE

"People are not good or bad—they are good and bad."

"People are funny; they spend money they don't have, to buy things they don't need, to impress people they don't like."

PREJUDICE

"Some idiots think they are thinking when in reality they are merely re-arranging their prejudices."

"As an unprejudiced person I will, with an open mind, listen to his bigoted lecture which I'm convinced is pure rubbish."

"A pessimist is a person who suffers sea-sickness on the entire voyage of life."

PERFECTION
"It takes less time to do a thing right than it does to explain why you did it wrong."

PURPOSE
"Everyone is of some use, even if nothing more than to serve as a horrible example."

PERSPECTIVE
"These are the good old days we will be longing for a few years from now."
—*John Sutter*

PAUSE
"If you're too busy to stop and think, stop and think."

PEOPLE
"Certain leaders can tell you to go to hell and you'll cheerfully obey. Others can hardly tell you to go to dinner without making you mad."

PREACHING
"When I preach on heaven I look as heavenly as possible. When I preach on hell my regular face will do."

QUIP
"A rabbit hunter climbed through the fence with his gun cocked. He is survived by his wife, three children and one rabbit."

QUITTER

"To avoid being a quitter, get fired."

"The only thing worse than a quitter is the coward who is afraid to begin."

"The greatest calamity is not to have failed but to have failed to try again."

"The Christian life is like an airplane; when you stop, you drop."

QUALITY

"Only mediocre people are always at their best."
—*Somerset Maugham*

QUESTIONING

"Never put a question mark where God puts a period."

QUARRELING

"To interfere with the quarrels of relatives is to go through life without a friend."

"I hate a quarrel because it interrupts an argument."
—*G. K. Chesterton*

"A quarrel is ended when one refuses."

"Quarrels could not last long if there were not faults on both sides."
—*La Rochefoucauld*

QUESTION

"If you had it to do over would you fall in love with yourself?"

"Why are goods sent by ship called cargo, while goods sent by car are called a shipment?"

RETIREMENT
"A man could retire nicely in his old age if he could dispose of his experience for what it costs him."

REFUSAL
"Will power should be balanced with won't power."

REWARD
"The world's most disappointed people are those who get what's coming to them."

"Life gives most of us what we deserve but only the successful will admit it."

RIGHTEOUSNESS
"To walk the straight and narrow path is far better than to move in the best circles."

RELIGION
"The religion that makes a man look sick certainly won't cure the world."

RIGHTS
"No man has a right to all of his rights."
—Phillips Brooks

REVENGE
"Don't lay for your enemies or lie for your friends."

ROMANCE
"After man came woman and she has been after him ever since."

RELATIVES
"Some people have trouble naming a new baby. Others have rich relatives."

"Success is a wonderful thing. You meet such interesting relatives."

REFINEMENT
"Some people become so polished they cast reflections on everyone."

REST
"Early to bed and early to rise makes a man baggy under his eyes."

REPUTATION
"So live that after the minister has ended his remarks, those present will not think they have attended the wrong funeral."

"An honest confession may be good for the soul but it is hard on the reputation."

REFORMER
"A reformer is one who insists upon his conscience being your guide."

RESPONSIBILITIES
"It is easy to dodge our responsibilities but we cannot dodge the consequences of dodging our responsibilities."
—*Josiah Stamp*

RELIGIOUS
"I have always noticed that truly religious people are fond of a joke and I am suspicious of those who aren't."
—*Alfred North Whitehead*

SAFETY
"The most unsafe part of an auto is the nut that holds the steering wheel."

"To avoid that run down feeling, cross streets carefully."

SPEECH
"A great many people, like cats, lick themselves with their tongues."

"There is a difference between having to say something and having something to say."

"Many throw their brains into neutral and let their tongues rattle on at high gear."

"One reason why a dog is such a loveable creature is that his tail wags instead of his tongue."

SELFISHNESS
"Edith was a little country bounded on the North, South, East and West by Edith."

SINCERITY
"Always be sincere whether you mean it or not."

SPEAKER
"I was cut out to be a speaker all right, but I got sewed up all wrong."

"If a speaker cannot strike oil in the first twenty minutes, there is no need to keep boring."

"There are two types of speakers—one who needs no introduction and one who deserves none."

"Blessed is the speaker who when he finishes also stops talking."

"Some people are like old shoes—all worn out except the tongue."

"Some speakers are like gamblers—they don't have sense enough to quit while they're ahead."

"I'm like a double feature, not just a lousy speaker but good and lousy."

SERMON

"For a sermon to be immortal it need not be eternal."

"A sermon is something you would not go across the street to hear but you would go across the state to preach."

SUCCESS

"A success learns how to make hay from the grass that grows under other people's feet."

"Behind every successful man there is a woman constantly reminding him he's not so hot."

"Work faithfully for eight hours a day and don't worry; in time you'll become boss, work sixteen hours a day and have all the worry."

"The secret of success is still a secret to most."

"Success is making more money to meet obligations you wouldn't have if you didn't have so much money."

STATISTICS

"Statistics can be juggled to support anything—especially statisticians."

SALVATION

"Most people who plan to be saved at the eleventh hour, die at ten-thirty."

STUPIDITY

"It's queer how we never get too old to learn some new way of being stupid."

"Gum-chewing is more popular than reading good books because it's much easier to exercise the chin than the mind."

SNOBBERY
"A snob is one who wants to know those people who don't want to know him."

SELF-CENTEREDNESS
"Even the conceited has one virtue, he seldoms talks about other people."

SUFFERING
"Most people are quite content to suffer in silence, if they are sure everyone knows they are doing it."

SUICIDE
"The last thing I'd do is commit suicide."

STINGINESS
"Some people are so stingy they take the corner on two wheels to save tires."

SPITE
"If thine enemy offends thee, buy each of his children a drum."

SAINTS
"In the church there are two kinds of members—the saints and the ain'ts."

THOUGHTFULNESS
"Do something daily to make other people happy—even if that means leaving them alone."

TACT
"If one of us would get off this tricycle, I could ride it much better."

—Henrietta Mears

"Tact is the ability to close your mouth before someone else wants to."

"Tact is letting others have your own way."

TALK

"If a thing goes without saying, let it go."

"Some gossipers are like an ink blotter—they soak everything up but it comes out backward."

"The one rule for talking is the one carpenters use: measure twice, saw once."

"Foolish people are like buttons—popping off at the wrong time."

TRAGEDY

"What a spiritual calamity—a preying mantis' only son turned out to be an atheist."

"In one large church the choir murdered the anthem, the organist drowned the choir, the preacher butchered the English and the janitor smothered the congregation."

THRIFT

"If your outgo exceeds your income, then your upkeep will be your downfall."

TIME

"Time may be a great healer but it's no beauty specialist."

TROUBLES

"Troubles are like babies—the more you nurse them, the larger they grow."

"I have lived a long life and I have known lots of trouble but most of it never occurred."

"If life gives you a lemon just squeeze it and make lemonade."

"If you have troubles, come share them with me. If you don't have troubles, come share your secret."

TITHE
"Not only will a man rob God but he'll take an income tax-deduction on it."

TEMPER
"When your temper boils over you are usually in hot water."

"The measure of a man is the things it takes to get his goat."

THANKFULNESS
"If you can't be thankful for what you receive, be thankful for what you escape."

THINKING
"The brain is no stronger than its weakest think."

"When two men in business always agree, one of them is unnecessary."
—*William Wrigley*

TECHNOLOGY
"With new machines that handle numbers of fifteen digits, lay two thousand bricks a day, and shell fifteen tons of peas, a man is a fool ever to get out of bed."

TRUTH
"No man has a good enough memory to be a successful liar."

UNCERTAINTY
"Certainly life expectancy is increasing. Now days you can expect anything."

UNKINDNESS

"Hardening of the heart ages people more quickly than hardening of the arteries."
—*Franklin Field*

UPBRINGING

"Let every father and mother realize that when their child is three years old, they have done more than half they will ever do for its character."
—*Horace Bushnell*

UNDERSTANDING

"If misunderstood don't worry. If unable to understand, start worrying."

"How lucky we are that people don't fully understand us. They couldn't stand it."

"I do not agree with a word you say but I will defend to death your right to say it."
—*Voltaire*

"Everywhere wives and husbands have at least one thing in common, to see each others faults."

"That young married couple had only one thing in common—they couldn't stand each other."

"Believe me, every man has his secret sorrows, which the world knows not; and oftentimes we call a man cold when he is only sad."
—*Longfellow*

"If we could read the secret history of our enemies, we would find in each man's life, sorrow, and suffering enough to disarm all hostility."

"The mind is like the stomach. It is not how much you put into it that counts, but how much it digests."
—*A. J. Neck*

VOCATION

"A scissors-grinder is the only person whose business is good when things are dull."

VACATION

"Religion is not a fur coat to be put away in moth balls during the summer months."

"The thrill of getting back home is by far the most enjoyable feature of a summer vacation."

"A vacation is recreation preceded by anticipation and followed by recuperation."

"Vacations for mothers are when boys go to summer camp."

VISION

"A teacher or preacher without a great vision will end up dreaming troubled dreams."

VALUES

"The world has forgotten in its preoccupation with Left and Right, that there is also an Above and Below."

"When a man is born people say, 'How is the mother?' When he marries they say 'What a beautiful bride.' When he dies they say, 'How much did he leave her?'"

"Without bread a man does not live long. If bread is all he gets, he cannot live well."
—*R. F. Auman*

"When mentioning things you can't afford, remember to include pride, envy, and malice."

VENTURING

"Behold the turtle: He makes progress only when he sticks his neck out."
—*James Conant*

VANITY

"A man wrapped up in himself makes a very small bundle fit to be tied."

VOTE

"Bad officials are elected by good citizens who do not vote."

WORK

"To get a job done, give it to a busy man. He'll get his secretary to do it."

"To live like a king means most of us must work like a slave."

"If you have time to kill, try working it to death."

"Baby-sitting meets a crying need."

"Remember when they didn't have to use 'Men Working' signs. You could tell they were working by watching them."
—*Tode Tuttle*

"People unafraid to roll up their sleeves seldom lose their shirts."

WIFE

"Maybe it's a man's world but the chances are it's in his wife's name."

"When I discovered my wife's mind ran in a different channel from mine, I bought another TV."

WEAKNESS

"Some people can resist everything except temptation."

WISDOM

"Most of us know how to say nothing; few of us know when."

WAR

"In an atomic war, all men will be cremated equal."

"Let us have peace on earth even if we have to fight for it."

WORRY

"Worry is like a rocking chair—it will give you something to do but it won't get you anywhere."

"Worry must help! What I worry about seldom happens."

"Oh, for a return of the early thirties when about the only major worry we had was the fear that we might starve to death."
—*Olin Miller*

WOMEN

"Women can keep a secret as well as men can, but it takes more of them to do it."

"There's only one way to handle a woman. The trouble is nobody knows what it is."

"Women have a wonderful instinct about things. They can discover everything except the obvious."
—*Oscar Wilde*

"Women's styles may change, but their designs remain the same."
—*Oscar Wilde*

"God created women beautiful and foolish: beautiful so that men would love them, foolish so that they would love the men."

"A wife's clothes either make or break her husband."

"God first created the universe and rested; then He created man and rested; finally He created woman and rested; since then neither God nor man has rested."

"If the President continues to appoint lady ambassadors, this country will always have the last word."

"You can never tell about a woman, and if you can, you shouldn't."

"Many a man enjoys going to church with his wife on Sunday, because he knows someone else is going to do the talking."
—Glen Preston Burns

"Women will remain the weaker sex just as long as they're smarter."

WAR

"The last war brought a lot of displaced persons; the next war will bring a lot of dis-personed places."

WHISKEY

"Whiskey makes you see double and feel single."

WISHING

"Many of us spend half our time wishing for things we could have if we didn't spend half our time wishing."

"The itching sensation which many mistake for ambition is merely inflammation of the wishbone."

WEALTH

"Wealth may not bring happiness but it helps you choose your favorite kind of misery."

"They claimed they were married by the Justice of the Peace, but it seemed like it must have been the Secretary of War."

"He was the kind of salesman that could sell an Eskimo a refrigerator."

"The tragedy of Noah was that of being in a boat in such a body of water with only two worms."

"Frustration is like a woman putting on her bra backwards and not knowing the difference."

"I'm from a long line of born losers. Soon after my grandfather bought an expensive cemetery plot, he took a voyage abroad and was drowned at sea. My father lost his hearing a week after he bought a stereo. My brother won a color TV but he was color-blind. I guess if I were to buy a pumpkin farm, Halloween would promptly go out of style."

"Often a bachelor has no buttons on his shirt. A married man often has no shirt."

"To speak ill of others is a dishonest way to praise ourselves."

"It is not a sin to be rich, it's a miracle."
—*Will Durant*

"Of course I'm head of my house. My wife is the neck but as you know, the neck turns the head."

"I ain't never made but one mistake in my whole life, and I see when I done it and taken it back."

"Many who claim they were tripped actually stumbled over their own feet."

"Tell a man there are two billion stars in space and he'll believe you, but if a sign says "fresh paint' he'll make personal investigation."

"A good neighbor is a fellow whose garden you can view with anticipation instead of jealousy."
—*Burton Hillis*

"Nothing is worse for those who have business than the friendly visits of those who have none."

"For a person as great as I am, it's difficult to remain humble."

"One principle guides me. I never strike a man when he is down. I always kick him."

"Before passing judgment on a sermon be sure to try it out in practice."

"When it's finally settled something can't be done, start watching for someone doing it."

"By laws of aerodynamics a bumble bee can't fly but the bumble bee has never grasped the law."

"We all agreed she should have buried her talent for plain speaking."

"A praying knee and a dancing foot seldom grow on the same leg."

YOUTH

"To stay young associate with youth. To die prematurely try to keep up with them."

"We all recognize adolescent youth. They begin to answer questions they themselves have been asking."
—*J. V. Jansen*

"To recapture youth, cut off his allowance."

"At adolescence, children stop asking questions because they know all the answers."
—*Jeanne Opalach*

"Growing up is the period spent in learning that bad manners are tolerated only in grown ups."

"Adolescence is that period when children tell their parents the facts of life."

"Adolescence is that period of life when children refuse to believe that someday they'll be as dumb as their parents."

YAWN

"A yawn may not be polite but it is at least an honest opinion."

"We open our mouths and yawn, hoping others will close theirs."

"He who has been taught only by himself had a fool for a master."

"The dictionary is the only place where success comes before work."

"People who growl and bark at others deserve to lead a dog's life."

"In the long range movement toward progress, a kick in the pants sends you farther along than a friendly handshake."
—*David Sarnoff*

"I've constantly watched that lazy guy for half a day and he hasn't done a stroke of work."

"The one time a woman isn't an angel is when she is up in the air and harping on something."

"To make a mistake is human but to keep repeating it is stupid."

"The most dangerous thing in the world is to try to leap a chasm in two jumps."
—*David Lloyd George*

"The only thing many children learn at their mother's knee is to watch out for cigarette ashes."